Live Canon

New Poems for Christmas

First Published in 2015
By Live Canon Ltd
www.livecanon.co.uk

All rights reserved

© Live Canon 2015

978-1-909703-08-7

Live Canon

New Poems for Christmas

Contents

All Apologies
Barney Norris

We are never where we ought to be.
Either the day is spent on the road

from house to house, glancing
into one life then another,

or you surrender and root yourself
in one place at the cost of all

the rest. But what does that say
about love? The long week pouring

into the year's turning takes the form
of a suite of apologies, unexpressed

but liquid in the air as the visits
knock on into Boxing Day, into New Year.

Christmas Eve
Doreen Hinchliffe

Midnight. A tabby slinks across the backs,
his fur smoothed by the wind. He slakes his thirst,
moves on. Now's the time insomniacs
like me sip tea, stargaze, wait for the first
grey streak of dawn to light the cobalt sky.
Upstairs, my child fights sleep, hoping to see
a host of eager reindeer flying high
above the roofs. I stand beside the tree,
step over piles of presents stretching far
beyond its branches. Reaching up, I prick
my finger on its pines, wish on its star,
long for a sudden snowfall inches thick
and sense a mystery turning in the air,
like tiny threads of gossamer, angel hair.

Seasonal Sonnet
Mab Jones

An elbow in the rib cage and I know
the time of tinselled tosh is drawing near;
all that glitters can and will be sold, and so
we battle in the streets each year.
A young mum runs her buggy o'er my toes,
her yowling brat blows snot as green as sprouts;
a gran slams past so fast she overthrows
a man who swears at me and starts to shout,
thinking I'm the cause. This is the season
of sleigh bells, brawls, and stabbings at the till;
the time of year we lose all sense of reason,
buying gifts with love, wishing we could kill
half the population, when they're in our way –
forgetting why we fete this bloody, blessèd day.

BJ Goes AWOL
Aileen la Tourette

for Reuben

Hey, you want this paper? Not at all.
Glad to pass on the bad news. Hey,
don't you think this mall's a lot like hell?
Five levels of concrete, instead of circles –

Never mind. Hey, you know where
the word *mall* comes from? England.
Mallets, balls, croquet on green lawns,
roads with trees on both sides. Nice.

This is a sinking ship. In dry dock.
It isn't rats leaving, it's gods. Look
at that crèche. Do you see Baby Jesus
in the manger? Nope. A dent in the straw,

almost like it was meant. A shape
you could trace, an emptiness saying
God is dead? At least *BJ went AWOL*.
Who blames him? Eternity means perfume,

cheap knockoffs even. No gold, incense,
myrrh. No, he split right out from under
Mary's ice-chip grin. Old Joe's stoical,
as always. It's his MO. Some poor guy jumped

off the fifth level, last week. Took the Fifth,
ho, ho, ho. Bet he was like old Joe, you know?
They're the ones. Don't say a word, just go.
Hey, maybe the guy who checked out grabbed BJ

on his way up the escalators? For company?
'Course it could've been some kids on Ritalin.
But I see that poor slob clutching the BJ doll
like Paul Newman with the football –

Cat on a Hot Tin Roof? Doesn't ring a bell?
Your IQ drops ten points in malls, goes on
dropping as you shop. No offence. He stops
at the Luau, twirls the little parasol in his cocktail,

stands up, walks over and drops himself
like a bomb. Long way down. Time to think.
Maybe he talks to BJ: Hey, *you're not Baby*
Jesus, you're baby me. Baby me! Wait, maybe

you're baby us – baby us, please, a mall prayer,
kinda says it all? Yeah, that's all bull. Hey,
they'll find another rubber doll, I guess
in one of those kid stores like Toys R Us?

Homage
Mark Huband

There is no time now, where once the bluebell
    stream bore tomorrow's
    promise of today.

Time has wrung brush boughs dowsed by stone-clad cold,
    capturing in ice
    all that lovers say.

My homage is to the promise I made,
    at the place we loved
    where the crows now bray.

All gone, the time, the place, where our love played
    beneath winter's trees,
        where the last light strays
        on the winter's freeze.

Christmas Ghosts
Natalie Scott

The blue spruce full of sap
stands spinous and strong

trees are brown skeletons
bolstered by the wheelie bins

The angel balances delicately
on the branch, dress immaculate

angels are packed flat,
dresses up over their heads

The stocking drips expectancy
over the hearth with its thimbleful

stockings are folded and flaccid,
thimbles supped and lipstick-marked

The cracker is heavy to hold,
promising something silver and useful

crackers are sloughed snake skins
with a tang of spent silver fulminate

The latest console rests potent in its box,
full of adventures, stories, other worlds

broken pieces spill over the curb,
adventures had and now old news

The latest console rests potent in its box
The cracker is heavy to hold
The stocking drips expectancy
The angel balances delicately
The blue spruce stands spinous and strong.

Mittens on a String
Ali Lewis

These cartoon ghosts,
lobster claws,
this telephone
of string between
cupped hands,
the fuzzy line
it traces
limb to limb,
this oath of warmth
our fingers form,
this slender
backwards hug,
this gesture,
clumsy as it is,
these proffered hands,
my Christmas gift.

Holidays
William Wyld

Out there the boulders roll quietly
into your path at night, tripping you up,
tearing out the guts of cars,
disturbed by animals you've never seen.
Let's go. Leave this damp winter behind for a week.
Two weeks. To where there's no way through
the baked sharp undergrowth, and after hours of climbing
black pines still block the view and there's
nowhere to go but back down and the sweat
pours off you, armoured horseflies swarm
and the faster you run the more you sweat
and the sweeter you smell
and the more the flies come.

Let's go, just a few days, and stay locked
in the high walled house with the black gates
under the blue wall of sky where men
crouch and squint in the heat, and vipers shift
the dead leaves, black, white, black.
Come, I'll show you the streams in the plains
that run dry half the year, pumped out
to feed the new hotels and the airport,
I'll show you where there used to be fish,
where the chemicals drain off the fields,
and whores stand in ones and twos
in the lay-bys and under bridges
the banks are strewn with everything
you can think of.

Two days. We'll walk past the acres
and acres of dry raked clods, a thousand
different blinding greys, on the white roads
that burn the insides of your eyes,
and four litres of water will last you

just half a day. Come, just half a day,
we can see the fences holding the dogs
trained furious by penniless men
with old rifles behind rusting mesh,
who sit and burn their cabins' roof timbers
in the night on broken-backed chairs,
leaving piles of dirty ash, white, black, white,
waiting hours for a beast to shoot.

Just an hour. To the streets crammed with people
screaming their throats raw waving
flags, striped, slashed, white, red, black
and the horses foam and panic in the din
and the riders are thrown before they've
even begun and after a hundred false starts
designed to run every beast through
with terror they drive them full tilt
round bends into barriers, snapping
tendons and bones and the winners
are gods and the dead horses are mourned
for five minutes. Five minutes. Stay here,
I'll tell you what it's like.

Stocking Fillers
Kirsten Irving and Jon Stone

i. Coal

A snowman's plucked eye,
a fire nest's dislodged egg.
Stubby underworld agent
who vanishes in the crowd.
Coal, you're a born tumbler,
bunker to scuttle to hearth
to skin you bright with dust.

ii. Selection Box

Choose me, Pigtails.
A cigar of a bar
stubborn with fudge.

Choose me, Roller Skates.
Soft from central heating,
caramel melting.

Choose me, T-Rex.
A bag that is air
and air and there a sweet.

Choose me, Banana.
Stick-you peanuts
and a crust of rippled cocoa.

Choose me, Gossip.
Jelly thumblets.
Crystalled with sugar.

Choose me last, Worryball.
One vicious bite
and I'll shatter into sticks.

iii. Wooden Soldier

Mercenary, partisan or deserter –
young, headlong from a skirmish.
His gloss the gloss of shined boots,
of blood, of a new glass *consolador*.

iv. Orange on Silver

Space bomb
out of space
out of wardrobe
out of stockings
take my key
take my filth away
peel the stash of magazines
the clinging pith
the parasite segment
the squirt
and leave my family
a ripe, respectable body.

Recipe for Christmas
Jenna Plewes

Ingredients

One well ripened aunt
a couple of grandparents
a handful of unexpected visitors
four assorted children
a large family dog.

Method

Soak the aunt in a pot of her favourite tea
add the grandparents and leave
to soften. Season the visitors
with crumbled mince pies
and alcohol of your choice.
Put the children in front of the telly
wrapping paper in the recycling

leave the mixture at room temperature
while he takes the dog out and you
lay the table, don't forget
to drink your first glass of wine.
Put the visitors on one side
with a hint of desperation.
Stir together the rest of the ingredients
and place around a meal you prepared
before anyone got up this morning.

This should be served with plenty
of jokes, party hats, drinks and laughter
it will feed an average family

for at least a week. Any left-overs
should be turned into bubble and squeak
by the person who wakes up first
after the repeat of the Queen's speech
at 6 p.m. and before the cartoons.

The Forgetful
Gillie Robic

At the ever-open minimart they curse their party shoes,
hobble along the winking shelves in panic
for milk, toilet paper, budgie seed and booze.

Wrapped in his habit a boy craves and mumbles
at a man buying six-packs, wine and whisky,
who shakes his head, pockets his change and stumbles

out, to window-framed trees glittering a fairy tale
of families leaning together around pretty presents.
Music booms, colours flicker and bleep, sirens wail.

Blockbuster movie mayhem and special FX stream
through the city, a World of Warcraft online
across the globe, changing levels of texture and dream.

On a bed of grease and torn crackers a carcass glistens
beside a flamed-out pudding. The telly reruns carols,
the Queen's christmas message, no-one listens.

Cats recoil from the riffraff, dogs scratch for the night.
Rats skulk under cars, in gutters and corners.
Foxes jellyroll in and out of the lamplight.

This christmas night is relatively free of danger.
Sponsored streets twinkle. The church locks up
ox and ass, the Holy Family, Jesus in a manger.

When They are Both Full Grown
Christopher North

It was in full swing with the yule log blazing,
the smell of roasting chestnuts,
Camilla being silly under the mistletoe
and Auntie Grace in spout about how many
berries she has on her ornamental holly.
The blur of people in our country kitchen
were opening and shutting the new units
with their crafty placement of death-watch
flight holes that look absolutely authentic
(Marisa's little man did them with a tiny drill),
I was pouring a rather grapey Chardonnay
for the new people from 'Woodland Edge'
and was in mid sentence with a story
about the hedge-laying we'd had done at the front
when Kate materialized and was tugging my arm:
'What is it?' I said through a clenched smile.
'You must come, you must come' she replied simply.
With a wave at the Simpsons who were admiring
that imitation Grinling Gibbons ivy in the hall,
I followed her to the conservatory.
'Look' she said.

Outside the trees were shrinking.
The beeches, the cherries, the Japanese maple
the Turkey oak, the balsam poplar;
shrinking with sighs as quiet as snow falling.
Shrinking into themselves,
the Arborvitae, the mountain ash;
becoming low, ground hugging,
like those ancient northern birches
that live through three month nights
under ice storms and pitiless blizzards,
flattening themselves into crevices and lees
never more than inches off the freezing wastes
of Iceland, Novaya Zemlya and the Arctic tundra.

The Donkey
Doreen Hinchliffe

They made my body out of bits of hessian,
stuffed me full of rags and stitched me round
with frayed threads pulled from the collar of a trench coat.

Two buttons from a shirt became my eyes
and bits of faded khaki my drooping ears.
My tail was the lock of a corporal's hair,
my legs – matchsticks dropped furtively
from the secret cigarettes of guards
and stamped into the mud beneath the wire.

On Christmas Eve
they placed me carefully
beside the ox, its curved white horns
carved from a broken tooth.

I looked around the other figures –
shepherds garbed in the torn-off corners of a sheet,
tiny sheep with crumpled strips of bandage
stuck to their pillow-case coats,
an ageing father,
the grey strands of his beard unpicked
from the single blanket in the hut.

Only the mother had any hint of colour,
her robe a subtle shade of blue,
pure cotton from the handkerchief
an officer was sent before he died.

That night and all next day,
the soldiers gathered round and sang.
A few stood in silence,
bowing their heads to a baby
that, like us, was forged from rags.

By early spring
the camp was closed,
the war now almost over.
The prisoners took away
the figures round the crib,
displayed them in the crypt
of San Imbroglio, Milan,
where still they stand, each one,

apart from me, that is.
They left me here, alone,
a testament to all the men
who stood beside me, once,
on Christmas Day,
but never made it home.

A Room in the City
Paul Carney

My hands know every nubble of the wallpaper.
The wind still shuffles about behind the fireplace.
On better days, I go downstairs for dinner;
tomorrow we shall have paper hats – it's Christmas
on television. We carried up the angled lamp
to stand it by my bed, bending above the pillow.
The rooftops opposite, the aerials, the stunted trees
like broccoli, forming my skyline are the same

but farther off. The birds that come and go
are more like shadow puppets now,
and never call my name across the street.
I may look out at half past three,
my head upon the windowsill, to watch
a tangerine and silver sunset.
Or I may not.

So many of the books I learned to read
in my cocoon of eiderdown and blankets
are here, lined up and leaning on the shelves. Today,
I took one down and opened it, and every page
was white. I think of all the letters I have known
dancing their spider-conga down in the narrow space
behind the cupboards. The phone rings in two rooms,
and I am not afraid; I know it won't be anyone for me.

I close this book. I lie here, until teatime,
stare up at the light-bulb, watch the plankton
drifting in the fishbowl of my eye, and half my head
is in and out of dreams; a man stands on the iron bridge
and shouts, and points to stars that are not there. How small
he looks from here. The clowns are crawling on the roof

and laughing in the chimney. Pigeons flap in empty rooms,
the starfish hands of children wave through clouds reflected
in the windows of a long white car, and on a beach, a woman
rolls in the surf, an arm flops from a floral-patterned sling,
and snow is falling on the tracks, and on the sea,
covering all the broken wooden boats
in silence. And someone on the wall calls out
to ask me what I know. But I am gone, already.

The central heating clanks all through the house.
The tumble drier is growling, down in the kitchen,
and in the next room, someone moves about, and sings along,
off-key, with *The Seekers' Greatest Hits*.
I am a child, sitting up in bed, pressing
my ear to the wall.

Everyman's Land
Christmas 2014
Mark Fiddes

We arrive stubbled from Friday night, legends of the club queue,
bhaji breathed, sweating Jager bombs and half-believing
our jackal tales of small town madness and the tongues of sirens.

Across the municipal scrub, the pitches have already surrendered
to fog and mud: our goalmouths are cratered and pocked with studs,
no demarcation, only the smudged white curse of the penalty spot.

All season these posts have stapled our hope into their orange nets,
snagged with tape and glory and drubbings by gigantic policemen
and Fancy Dans in feather cuts and newly released psychopaths.

We should pray but between us we have too many Gods.
Profanely, we struggle into boots still caked with last Saturday,
as luminous as grubs in laudromat green, our numbers peeling.

Never will we feel as mighty as this, with burning rubber
anointing our brows from a field away where they have filled the land
with chromed caravans, frozen washing and the opera of dogs.

Destiny turns up, hooped in maroon and blue from the car park
along the cinder track at a slow clop, bowed as regimental horses
under a saddling of first aid, spare balls and crates of Lucozade.

With only three shopping days to Christmas we rise as warriors
to bellow the only verse we know of *Oh Come All Ye Faithful*
complete with hand gestures and miracles as yet unborn in our feet.

The Rocking-Horse Christmas
Doreen Hinchliffe

The air smelt different when I woke –
the scent of Santa Claus, perhaps,
or reindeer fur, or maybe the lingering
hint of stardust in the hearth.

A bolster-case bulged and beckoned,
a pillow-case too, the corner of a blue box
jutting out through the flap at its top.

Desperate for mam and dad to come and look,
I scrambled up and headed for their room.

It was there, on the landing, I saw him first.

Twice my height, he stood
like the steed of a prince in a fairytale,
his red saddle asking to be mounted,
his thick black mane waiting to be stroked.

Stock still, hardly daring to breathe,
I gazed up at his immense frame –
the dappled black and white of his body,
his partly-open mouth set in a wide smile,
the deep dark eyes that fixed me in their gaze
and claimed me as their own.

Dad hoisted me up
and pushed me slowly to and fro,
retreating once I gained the confidence
to let my arms unclasp themselves
from round the horse's neck.

Then, with knees thrust hard into his sides
and both feet jammed in his stirrups,

I leaned my body forward and pulled back,
yanking the reins with both hands
till his head rocked up and down, up and down,
higher and lower, higher and lower,
the two of us locked in an airborne embrace.

All day we galloped together,
careered across the heather-covered moors,
raced through magic woods and hidden glens,
leapt over fences and fast-flowing streams.

All day we galloped
as if nothing mattered,
as if we two alone existed,
we two, flying as one
with the wind in our hair
and the thunder of earth beneath our feet.....

the bolster-case abandoned,
the pillow-case untouched.

The Cord
Mark D. Cooper

for Liz

It was the Christmas when Mandela died.
We huddled round the TV while our grief
for our own lost elder unfolded in the back bedroom.

Greetings cards in the window that read 'Grandson'.
Half a pack of cigarettes on the table.
An advent calendar with most of the doors still closed.

They're in the village where Mandela's umbilical cord
is buried. "The mood here: very joyful," says the report.
Rain from the storm grounding flights across the Irish Sea
shatters the light from warm windows across the street.
A neighbour calls round to tell the story of a dream
in which her dead husband will be married to Christ.
"That's fucking mental," says your auntie's old boyfriend.
Maybe, but even in loss there is a kind of gain.
You're finally sleeping in your Moses basket.
One day, you may dig in the garden your grandad kept,
find your connection to this fertile ground.

Christmas Post
Hilary Watson

It all started with a banana –
about six inches
with a bend. A friend
asked *May I…?*
And *Of course*,
I said.

She placed it on the scales
in the Post Office.
First Class, please.

But it isn't packaged.

   The skin is the packaging

You can't send that!
   The woman's flashing antlers
wobbled as she shook her head.

Two days later, three stamps,
the address in biro,
it arrived through my letter box

with an apology from the Royal Mail
for my damaged property.

I gleamed. Sent a piece of toast,
stamps, address in Tip-Ex
to my green grocer friend.

To stem a cold, she mailed
a handkerchief, embroidered
with instructions
inside a self-addressed
orange.

For Christmas, I dealt a pack of
playing cards to friends
and family, one-by-one.

Chase the Ace. The grocer
found the Joker late,
but I got rid of my whole hand.

I posted
stationery
in exchange for letters,
scorched
chess pieces
to enemies,

unpackaged books
as gifts
with marked front covers.

Eventually, Royal Mail caught on.
Return to Sender
my Judas.
I was blacklisted. Sent by the courts
for counselling.

While the shrink
scratches his head, I say

My father once received two
lizards in the post, from Bath.

He lifts his head,
the pencil staining his hand
where the address has bled.

I hear you can write a cheque
on a cow and cash it.

He lowers his gaze,
Starts scribbling.

For the Lady
Geraldine Clarkson

This old December, let ice shingle
in the eaves, let frost sparkle
on the ground, sprinkle diamonds
in the fields. Let skies in the dark
wink with stars. For the Lady.

Let winter earth break open,
heavy clay fall away,
rock, crust, and mantle, crack:
bud forth an Infant. Let flinty
silence sing. For the Maiden.

See, she's kneeling by a Child,
folds her cloak around Him,
her immaculate breath mingles,
in the midnight warm-straw air,
with the Bairn's. Her bright Sun.

Clamber near the Crib,
jostle shepherds in the night;
tiptoe round the lolling oxen;
bring a candle to the Light.
Maybe He will smile. For the Lady.

So simple, so impossible
Jenna Plewes

all the creator's love
held in a trusting girl

while stars blaze
and every pebble sings.

Twelfth Night
Dino Mahoney

Stripped bare, peg-legged, balding,
dumped outside as whining vacuums
suck up clattering needles.
.
Those that threw them out
first waltzed them in,
dressed them in jewels,

draped them in pulsing lights,
crowned them with stars,
stacked gifts at their feet

and with shut eyes inhaled
the resin scent of fairy tale,
concrete melting into gingerbread.

Now, back to work,
shifty former hosts
look the other way

embarrassed by the line of amputees
sprawled along the street
strands of tarnished tinsel clinging on,

ashamed of the child
that took them in, the adult
that turfed them out.

New Year's Eve
Matt Bryden

Our dog has lost a claw.
We found it on the fireplace tiles
as it just lay there, turning a back
on all this turbulent housework.

Our red wine fizzed,
its notes having heightened
and fallen, lost complexity
below the drinking charts in the cellar.

Camilla opened the gate
and hooves crossed the yard
outside our study. I had a bag
in my black tea, she had her steak rare

with pepper. These days
we drink and drink but don't
get drunk. Lodged in the E.N.O.
while the R.O.H. crackles.

The date dial of my watch turns
at five minutes to. Its strap
is real leather. I can't stop
looking at its face.

LIVE CANON